TO

Becky

FROM

Gwen

DATE

A Birthday Blessing

WELLERAN POLTARNEES

NINETEEN HUNDRED *1998* AND NINETY-EIGHT

BLUE LANTERN BOOKS

FIRST PRINTING.

PRINTED IN SINGAPORE.

ISBN 1-883211-03-4

BOOK & COVER DESIGN:

SACHEVERELL DARLING AT BLUE LANTERN STUDIO

BLUE LANTERN BOOKS

PO BOX 4399 SEATTLE WASHINGTON

98104

To mark the anniversary of your birth, I send you this Blessing.

I hope that friends gather

to celebrate you, and I trust that

those who cannot be with you

find ways to tell you of their affection.

A *Birthday* Blessing

I here send you my loving wishes,

to add to the gifts, tangible

and intangible, that you have earned.

A *Birthday* Blessing

May you find, in your life's journey,

many pleasant places from which

to watch and enjoy the pageant

of existence – porches, window seats,
(especially Back Porches!)

nooks, river banks, bowers, balconies

and perfectly placed windows.

A *Birthday* Blessing

Let there be frequent

and fine conversations,

A *Birthday* Blessing

... and quiet times with friends,

when words are not needed,

and the rustle of leaves,

or the movement of water,

seems the central fact of existence.

A *Birthday* Blessing

May the wonder of creation

be ever before you.

A *Birthday* Blessing

M. Hasselriis

May there be ample opportunities

for you to create,

A *Birthday* Blessing

... and to enjoy the creations of others.

A Birthday Blessing

Make sure there are flowers everywhere

in your life – in your yard, at your door,

on your table, by your window.

A *Birthday* Blessing

I hope for you

rich and attainable daydreams,

A Birthday Blessing

... and night dreams in which you

adventure grandly, and reach both

understanding and solution.

A *Birthday* Blessing

Let there be plentiful books,

and the leisure to read them.

A *Birthday* Blessing

May there be many evenings

bright with lanterns,

A Birthday Blessing

... and many mornings rosy in

their beginnings and crystalline

in their fullness.

A *Birthday* Blessing

Let this birthday be an opening into a more glorious existence.

A *Birthday* Blessing

Would that I could give you infinite

birthdays and time unmeasured,

but instead I send you a sense of the

freedom from time that can be achieved

by those who fully embrace

each moment.

Picture Credits

Front Cover	Alexandra Day. "A Birthday Gift," 1998.
Endpapers	Fanny Brate. "Nameday," 1902.
Half-Title	Unknown. Postcard, n.d.
Frontispiece	Josef Engelhart, "The Wind," 1897.
Back Cover	Jean A. Mercier. Advertising poster, 1924.
4	Charles A. Winter. Magazine cover, 1908.
6	Gaston de Latouche. "L'Intrigue Nocturne," n.d.
7	H. Meserole. Magazine cover, 1923.
8	A.F. Gorguet. Magazine cover, circa 1896.
9	Edward Robert Hughes. "A Basket of Oranges," circa 1878.
10	Henri Le Sidaner. "La Table sous la Tonnelle," 1917.
11	Jean Mannheim. "Our Wisteria," circa 1912.
12	Harry Wilson Watrous. "Some Little Talk of Me and Thee There Was," 1916.
13	Louis Ritman. "Day Dreams," n.d.
14	C.R.W. Nevinson. Advertising poster, 1925.
15	Henri Lebasque. "La Terrasse," 1913-1914.
16	Frederick William Burton. "The Dream," n.d.
17	M. Hasselrils. Magazine cover, circa 1930's.
18	Carl Larsson. "My wife; Karin in the studio," 1912.
19	Joseph Kleitsch. "Problematicus," 1918.

Picture Credits